BY ZACH

UNDERWATER MOUNTAINS PUBLISHING
LOS ANGELES, CALIFORNIA
A SECRET COMPANY.

86 BY ZACHRY K DOUGLAS
EDITED AND ARRANGED BY VINCENT CONVERTITO

86

"86","86ed", "86'd", or eighty-sixed when used as a verb in American English, is a slang term for getting rid of something, ejecting someone, or refusing service. The phrase "80 miles out and 6 feet under" was reserved for someone who had to dig their own grave 80 miles from civilization and then get shot execution-style. All terms for 86'd originated from this.

before she died, she told me,

"do not look to the moon to see me,
do not look to the wind to hear me call your
name.
do not look to the oceans to feel me around you,
look only into your heart,
for i am going home now."

and with the final breath she drew,
my heart gradually grew in size;
filling all the emptiness that was
left behind by my soulmate saying
goodbye.

a heart that once only kept me alive,
now is forever holding her love inside.
my life is yours and i will live for you.

a life that now beats for two.

i have been thinking about you for a
while now and we need to talk.
i know and understand that there is
still love woven into the words in
which i speak that may scare you off.

but every time i pick up the phone,
i press end,
hoping i hit the button soon enough,
for i am afraid that there is no longer
love hidden in yours.

if i never get the courage to finally
see the call through, just know

I love you and want a life with
You and only you.

my soul and i need you to be whole
again. so if i call,

 please pick up.

it is important.

i imagine a life where souls
dance and stomp their feet
to the rhythm of a thousand
heartbeats. carelessly falling
in love with another soul;
just to feel alive. a place
so divine, no human is allowed
inside.

i feel like i was not made
for this place.
maybe the universe made a
universal mistake.
my soul is too young for these
young humans and their childish
games.
-the many faults of a human-

when i close my eyes to kiss
you, it is more than just to
feel your lips.
i close them to see your soul.

for a minute, she thought she was
the moon with all of these
juvenile wolves howling
at her.

while in reality, she was
my universe;

collecting my kisses and creating
constellations on my heart
for my soul to look at.

i like to watch the stars
as the day draws to an
end.

not because i am looking
for the ones that are
falling, but more or
less thinking that
you are looking
down at me,

watching over us, as we
go through another day
without you.

maybe you talk amongst the
others and wish on us humans.
maybe you envy us as much as
we envy the brilliance of
you all.

i can only imagine what it is like
to have your love. how our souls
would runaway together and
never return.

far from this world's reality,
is where we would create our
own.

where you and i would go fishing
for stars and swim through the
black holes of eternity. being
lost in love with you is
what i need.

tucked away, in the corner of
my mind is where you will
stay. you will forever be there;
making love with my thoughts
and sleeping soundly with my dreams.

last night, i remembered how your
hands would write on my flesh.

you would inscribe your confessions
and darkest secrets on it. i loved
you for that.

trusting my soul with your desires
and nightmares, hoping that they
wouldn't bleed into me.

not only did those words seep into me,
your soul found solace in the arms of
mine.

as if they wanted to hold each other's
pain.

i finally found someone as
mad as me and she is
everything that chaos
has dreamt about.

for she stirred my soul with
her soulful hands and now we
are creating priceless art
for the stars to look at.

i kissed the moon
goodnight and she

felt it from a
world away.

all she wanted was to feel
human again, so he grasped
her hand and placed it over
his heart, telling her,

"this will beat for you
until the end."

i once lit my soul on
fire with the tip of
your tongue.

now the universe eternally
burns for only your love.

i will shed my soul to
cover your naked bones.
you are not different,
my love. you are a
gorgeous human and
you will never be
alone.

this deranged world will not
wreck you, nor will it steal
away a heart that has always
been my home.

that's why i am here.
to love you forever
and protect you from
it all.

as they say, "there will always
be more fish in the sea."
but to me, you were my catch.

i wanted to be selfish and keep
you all to myself.
now i know that i had to let you
go, for you needed the oceans.

they will always be your home
and i took you away from a life
that you loved.

and for that, i am truly sorry,
my dear.

you make me feel
like i can never
get close enough
to you.

as if our souls
were trying to
hold each other,
but our bodies
got in the way.

love can be a lonely
place.

try not to get lost
along the way.

all it took was her kiss
to melt all of my stars;
creating the moon in
my life.

the one that will always
guide me home in the
middle of my sleepless
nights.

as i placed my right hand
on the left side of my
chest, i can still
feel your lovely
heartbeat.

during my lonely nights,
when the world gets too
loud, i count them
to fall asleep.

she was a rebel who was born with
a fierce heart and wild soul.
i loved and respected her
for both, but i did not
want to confine her
vibrant spirit in
a fixated world.

you see, she desired to be the actual
bloom of life for those who were
content with merely being alive.

her smile set fire to the imagination
of reality; ultimately becoming
a trailblazer.

and i... all i wanted to do was
burn with her.

-freedom from my mind-

i have been beaten by your words.
strangled by your haunting curse.
spat on by your impassionate views.
mishandled and misused for the last
time by you.

accumulating a lifetime of abuse,
i shall kick in the door to an
island universe. i will swim
with the angels and submerse
my soul;
rising from the waters, revived
and whole.

and if life should ever
get in the way between
you and i,

i will attach our memories
to my heart, with just
enough string and fly
it in the sky for you
to always see;

wherever i go, you will
forever be a part of me.

my whole life, i have been
searching for the wrong thing.
i have been looking for my twin
flame, instead of finding the real
me.

to love you right and love you
forever, i will have to search
beneath the darkest of covers.
i will need you to guide me with
the light of your heart.

only then will i find my soul;
hidden beneath my old, lonely
and brittle bones.

I LIKE BEING ALONE.

crowds of people drive
anxiety through the roof.

MY WORLD. MY REALITY.

i keep the company that
allows me to stay grounded.

he was the misunderstood
kid that always had to
look over someone else's
shoulder to see the world.

now, he has matured into
a loving father who holds
his own child on his shoulders
just to understand life a little
better.

gripping your hands, i think i
finally have a grip on reality.

to me, drinking you in with every
moment we spend talking about how
the earth is not big enough for us both
is just what i need.

i blackout with your love. i forget
a wretched place even exists in our
universe.

you curse under your breath,
but you revel in what we have
created.

they told her, "why just be a star,
when you can be your own world.
there you can live and be everything
that you want to be; the stars. the
moon. the ocean. the sun."

"i've never looked at it like that."
she laughed and had a grin for miles
at the mere thought of the idea.
though in the end, it made her realize
that she did not have to be like everyone
else. you see, even stars fall for
empty wishes. wished on by those who
do not believe in the star itself;
only the light surrounding it.

from then on, she would be her own world.
creating a place so in tune with her
thoughts and ideas that all of those
would become her stars. her smile would
create the moon and her eyes, those
worldly beautiful eyes, they would create
the sun. her tears would create the
oceans and her breath would be the wind
allowing the breeze of love to pass
through all who wished on her stars.

i do not need all the
extravagant words to
impress you.
i just want to love
you for the rest of
my life.
even after my final
goodbyes come in the
form of my last breath,
i will wait for you
endlessly;
until our souls are
reunited again.

-soulmate-

where souls find true love
and
the right heart in humans.

just know what comes
from the heart has to
pass through the soul
first.

you ignorant fools,
all she ever wanted
was magic;

the kind she could
finally believe in.

undressing you with my eyes,
i see how big your heart
really is.

a heart of love;
now that's something worth
admiring.

i write for someone i have yet
to meet, yet she already knows
everything about me.

i see myself waking up next to
her for the rest of my life
and i cannot wait to fall
asleep tonight.

this time, i know that my muse
will be next to me, waiting for
moments to turn into memories.

it is finally our turn to just
be happy and not worry about
what never was.

from now on, it will forever be...
just us

just because it might
seem hopeless,

does not mean that we
should hope less.

i want to hold you like
no one else has before.
those who have tried
always failed to keep
you safe and whole.

their minds will never fully
comprehend the way the universe
holds the stars at night;
softly, peacefully and lovingly.

being held is a substantial part
of understanding a human.
somehow, we always let go too
soon or too late. though at
times, we are fortunate enough
to have everything fall into
place.

if you look to the sky at night,
the most perfect display of
devotion greets those who dare
to know the true meaning;
star by star.

you have never experienced
love,

until you have felt a smile
hold you in the middle of
the night.
i finally understand the
meaning of living in the
moment.

living in a moment with you
is better than living a
lifetime alone.

with an anxious look on her face,
she said, "i have shared my entire
life story with you. i bet you
think i am crazy or weird don't
you?"

as our souls locked hands, the only
thing i needed to say was, "no dear,
i find you to be human.
believe me when i tell you that's
a beautiful thing. all i ask of you
is this: never stop being yourself
around me. to lose you, i would
miss out on life itself."

she is the most exquisite
and magical flower of love
i have ever held in my
hands.

for the rest of my life,
i will constantly breathe
her in;
getting high off of her soul
and lost in her heart.

if it were not for
the mirror,
how would you see
yourself?

you were more than just magic,
my dear,
you were love itself.

my aching lips begged of yours
and my lonely heart spoke of
your name.

together, we would live amongst
the engulfing flames of which
we created.

sparked by the kissing of our
souls and forever bonded by the
stars that fell to watch us grow.

our life was far from perfect,
but we loved one another for
those precious moments when
we became each other's shoulder.

those times will always be a
pictured memory that hangs on
the walls of my soul.

so when i think that life is
getting too heavy to hold,
i close my eyes, take a
breath and realize just
how far we have come.

just to see you smile again,
my love, i will give you the
one that you gave to me.

the one that cured all of my
aches and pains.
the one that covers my face,
ear to ear.

that smile will never allow
fear to overtake me, nor will
it destroy the essence of my
belief.

for i believe in us and the
power of giving back to those
who have given everything to
me.

she has a taste for chaos and her
appetite for life is something i
often dream about.

she is fearless when it comes to the
difficult moments that this universe
continue to confront her soul with.

each day, she leaves me licking my
lips which are forever coated in
her magic; a reminder to me that
she will always be the angel who
gave me my wings.

for she saved a shattered spirit
and taught him not only how to
fly, but how to land without
ever looking down.

my eyes are filled with
memories of once before.

they speak for me when my
mouth can't find the words.

if you look deep enough,
you might be able to see
the curse;

when they try and close at
night, they stay open to
the universe.

always have an extra place
open and available in your
heart for those who are less
fortunate than you.

someday they will need a
place to stay.

to see a child smile amidst the
complete suffering of what our
planet is enduring truly is
a miracle.

i am amazed by the amount of
innocence that lives within
that special gift. for they
have no idea the world in which
they live and exist is the exact
same place we are trying to protect
them from.

to my unborn child, i will die
to keep you safe from any evil
that lurks amongst the shadows,
seen or unseen.

it is not my first broken
heart, nor will it be my
last.

i am good at being alone,
but it is nice to hold
someone's hand while
the rest of the world
sleeps.

when for a moment in time,
i had the world next to
me. she just didn't hold
my hand,

she held my soul perfectly.

she said, "i give up.
this damn world is too
cold, even for my warm
heart."

then her soul hugged her and
said, "not yet, dear. there is
more to life than worrying
about what others keep inside.
i need you to believe in me,
the same way i have always
believed in you. keep fighting."

i told her to take my hand
and show me where it hurt
the most.

to my astonishment, she took
my hand and placed it over
my own wounded heart.

you came into my life
when all i needed was
a smile from someone
who cared enough to
stay with me.

it saved my soul from the
depths i had taken it.
now i am able to see another
sunrise because of the
moment we made interlocking
our fears with the idea of
forever.

all it takes is a glimmer
of hope to transform a
tragedy into a beautiful
life.

with our love,
we kept the world
spinning;

allowing the stars
a chance at immortality.

your name still
echoes through
the cavities of
my lungs.

longing to cry
out and breathe
you again.

all i ask of you
is before you judge me,
understand the scars that
cover my heart.

they tell a story of an
intrepid soul who is
trying to piece together
a human with borrowed
parts from the stars.

if i told your lips a
secret,
could you keep them
closed?

we are the reflection of life and it
will always project the love not only
we need, but the love other humans
desire; humans who live on the streets,
asking for a dollar so they won't
freeze.

we are the reflection of life and i
hope that it is kind enough to give
to those who need more love than a
cardboard box can provide or a bridge
acting as a roof over their heads.

my wish in life is that one day i
can eventually give everything
i have just so others can experience
love. maybe not the word itself,
but clean sheets and a pillow,
served with hope and a side of
affection that goes beyond just
a dollar bill and some loose change.

your heart was a

song i once composed.

as i looked out of my second
floor window last night, my
wandering eyes got lost in
the enchanting skies like
they always do.

for the moon will always remind
me of you. wherever you go, it
will forever have your luminous
glow of life and love.

i know it will continue to share
the light that was created
inside of you. spending this
brilliant moment alone,
i am thankful for each
time the moon...

comes back home.

waking up, hungover on
love, is a feeling i can
never get enough of.

when our fingertips touch,
our souls begin to runaway
with each other;
to a place unknown to humans.

i regret

not having made

memories with

you yet.

every night, the stars mourn
and they cry out. for they
have lost one of their own
kind.

it was the night you fell
from the universe's grasp.
it was an intoxicating ride
to see you fall and land
right next to me.

now all the stars use their
powers to assimilate
their shine in your
eyes.

in the end,

it was love, that completely
destroyed their hearts.
it was forgiveness, that helped
pick up the pieces.
it was hope, that made it beat
again.
it was the soul, that empowered
them to find peace in a
broken heart.

she turned to me and
said, "hold me."

so i dropped my own world
i had been holding and
picked her up with both
hands.

together we experienced
what life is all about:
understanding.

love is not love, until
you have had your hands
full of your own problems,
only to realize that the
universe you are living
in was created by chaos.

-home-

where two souls cleanse

themselves with each other's

love.

after being tormented for
years, she used her poem
like a nickel plated .45;
murdering the devil on
her shoulder.

now she dances in his ashes,
like a young child running
through the rain.
soaking in all of the pleasures
he once took away.

what i would give,
just to taste you
again.

your skin was the sweetest
of all the forbidden fruit.

then for the dessert, i would
kiss your soul so deeply
that even it would be
speaking in tongues.

her heart was rough around
the edges, but it was a
diamond nonetheless.

one of which i could not
afford, but i always
managed to get lost
looking at it;

admiring the shine and trying
to understand the purity of
which it held.

you see, she did not need a ring
from someone to prove their love
to her. for she had everything
she could ever want on the
inside.

in the end, the value of self-worth
is priceless.

the love i have lost is the kind
that will never leave me.

my life story was perfectly made
from a beautiful tragedy.

always remember why you cared
and allow that passion to carry
you through to the next journey.
wherever that is, be happy that
you are allowed another opportunity
to live life filled with tiny
miracles every day.

your touch ignited all
the stars in my soul

creating a whole new
universe of feelings
i have never known
before.

i swear you could move
mountains with your
touch.

it is so powerful, i am
addicted to it, like
a soul jonesing for
love.

for i am a poor man's soul
with the richest of hearts
trying to survive in a world
where humans value wealth
more than they do love.

you are a special kind
of human.
one that carries a soul
that shines for others.

life is such an agonizing and
spirit wrenching place at times.
hell, even love teases you
with the possibility
of forever.

but i will continue to swim
against the current until
there is no more water to
tread.

with our naked hearts and
jubilant souls, we will
never again be divided
by two sides of the sea.

one day, the waves of hope will
finally rest on the shorelines
of love. that, my dear, is a
promise i will die trying
to keep.

i wake up every day thinking that
this will be the last breath i
will be able to take.

it's not the best way to live,
but it allows me to write with
a purpose.

second chances are hard to come
by, but i have been given more
than enough to understand that
my life is about living for those
in which death has visited...

when it should've been me.

my life is complicated;

like chaos meeting love
for the first time.

no matter how many
breaths i take...

i will love you until
the last one.

through the radiance
of your smile,

you showed me the way
to my soul.

the true measure of
a human is not the
size of their heart,
but how well they
comfort those in
need.

in my life, i have struggled
just to survive. it is a
complicated, yet delicate
story about a broken
home that helped
shelter a broken
soul.

sometimes i close my eyes,
just to find a new reality.
one where the horizon is
scattered between heaven
and hell.

as i constantly battle my
demons lurking in my thoughts,
the war rages on with my own
damn shadow.

these humans keep telling
me that smoking my cigarettes
and drinking my whiskey will
eventually kill me one day.

obviously they have never
missed you before, mi amor.

"i will take a dozen of those red roses."

right then, i knew what she was going to say. "you must me in trouble or are you going to surprise her?"

with my face turning a shade of red it seldom sees, i explained to her, "no, mam, i am not in trouble. i buy a dozen red roses every day to leave for her in a vase, so she can see just how much the flowers are jealous of her divine beauty."

she laughed and said, "that is something you don't hear all the time." shaking my head back and forth, i truthfully said, "well, dear, you've never seen her kind of magic before. i've seen it for 65 years and the best thing about it is our love has kept us alive. no water needed. just love."

if i wait for you, will you stand
in the rain with me and drink the
dreams coming down from the heavens?

if you will, then we shall get drunk
off of the understanding that love
is nothing more than waiting a
lifetime to die with your soulmate;
only to be born again in the next
life.

wait with me and i swear i will live
in your arms forever; making love to
every inch of the naked emotions and
hidden secrets that we will share
together. wait for me and i will never
leave your side. not even time will be
able to tell us to leave this world.

for we are the makers and keepers of
what we have created. we were born
to hold each other, so that we would
never have to die alone.

i will shape my spine to
fit the contours of your
soul.

i want to experience what
it is like to forever
live in you.

all you have to do in
life is run when they
tell you to walk and
you will be just fine.

i have craved you,
ever since you
made my soul
speak of
love.

i took this black ink you
now read from the tattoo
you once had on your arm
that made-up our sleeve.

it now tells a story of a
man who is heartless because
a woman he once loved stole
it and sold it for diamonds.

somehow, she could never
understand that only a
heart of love lasts forever.

always know this, darlin',
my story will never be more
important than yours.

together, we will have the
universe giving us a standing
ovation, while it allows us
to have a sky full of stars
all to ourselves.

she was born with the
light of the moon
inside her soul.

for it was just as
bright and beautiful
as her natural glow.

i will never forget the time
cancer took you away from me.
it was the night all of my
stars died, trying to bring
you back to life.

so i cried. wishing that my
tears falling from my pain-ridden
eyes could somehow make an ocean
of memories in which i could always
go to...

just to see you wash ashore and
hold my hand to let me know
that it is ok to swim again.

she did not have the passion
to fit in or be of the normal
type. her fire was out of control,
aiming to be the crazy and wild
kind.

all i could do was stand back
with my eyes forever locked
with hers;
hoping our flames could dance
all over the moon.

together, we created a life that
would burn in any world.
for the rest of our lives,
we shall live as if death will
never be able to find us.

there is no such thing as
the last time with you.
everything we do is and
will always be the first
time for me.

loving you makes sense to
my soul and that is all
the proof i need to
realize everything
before you was in
preparation for us.

i can honestly say now, i am
thankful for all the heartbreaks,
angst and misery i went through.

without it, i never would've
found you for the first time.

i once gave you the
flower of my soul
to place in the
window of your
heart.

to this day, it has
continued to grow
with petals made
of memories that
will never wilt
away.

all it needs is the right
amount of love.

if you want to know me, then i will
tell you something nobody knows.
my life was a father coming home for
christmas, arriving in his black
toyota truck, full of presents for my
brothers and me.

life for me was two days later when he
had to leave again for work in order to
make back the money he had spent on three
boys who thought santa was real.
before he left, you could see me running
out into the driveway, crying to myself,
begging him not to leave again.

my life was complicated because i felt so
much anger and love at an early age.
sometimes i close my eyes and i can still
see that young boy with his hands waving
in the air to bring his father back.

my life is full of stories that i have
kept inside. but what's the point of
that when you're not helping anyone?

tell your story and let it burn within the
hearts and souls of others. you might just
end up saving someone tonight.

to go through life knowing
i'll never be able to touch
you in the places still
buried deep beneath your
soul

will always be a tragedy i
never knew could exist with
someone who they have yet
to hold.

but i guess that's what
dreams are for.

before she had ever met me, the sky
was her first true love. so i painted
her with the colors from up above.

i used all of the fiery reds and
pinks that i could find. for her
eyes were made with so much love
and light.

the kind that could keep any canvas
filled with eternal sunshine.

when we touched, we connected
our hearts with the stars;

providing a universal night light
for all of those who were
left alone and broken
in the dark.

in life, when you know it is
real, you will never be able
to hide love.

always remember that every
human has seen it,
but not every soul has felt
it.

she said she was broken
and that love couldn't
fix her.

so i showed her my heart
stitched and how love
put me back together.

her world did not revolve around
the fairy tales or the fantasies
that other got lost in.

for her world was centered on
love and love only though she
knew what could happen if she
gave too much.

in her eyes, love was the only
thing that was real and it was
always more than enough for me.

while trying to find
yourself,

do not get lost in the
shadows behind you.

i would literally give
you my spine,

if that could finally
make you stand up
for yourself.

i had this conversation last
night and asked her how many
pillows does she sleep with.
she said none and then asked
me the same question.

"i sleep with one and keep
another one next to me.
i've always kept an extra
pillow on that side. just
a habit i guess.
sometimes, it's nice to think
someone is using it to dream
with me."

though i may not be as
happy as i was once
before,

i know i will find
happiness again.

it has always been so much
more than just sex for me.
i am a romantic, so
everything is fair
game.

i want a woman who will walk
with me on the beaches when
it is raining and not worry
about the storms at sea.

i would rather make love to
the sounds of waves
crashing than i would
a favorite song.

the universe is my playlist
and you are the notes that
i hear...

every single day.

i would literally give
you my spine,

if that could finally
make you stand up
for yourself.

she asked me, "do you still
want to go, babe?"

with this dumbstruck look on
my face, all i could get out
of my mouth was, "well, dear,
that was four whiskeys ago."

never knowing exactly how thirsty
my soul was for a glass of firewater,
by time i finished my last drink,
i needed another one. she left with
disgust and me and jack discussed
life. mainly the irony of a drunken
thought.

i go to bed and sleep with my
fingers tightly crossed.
praying i wake up tomorrow in
a world that understands hope
and accepts dreams as currency.

her love was laced with ecstasy
from the stars. a universal
overdose was felt throughout
my entire world.
for i could not resist the
temptation of her celestial
kiss.
once our lips started talking,
i could feel the rush and
overpowering sensation of
her magic.
her body danced with the devil,
while her soul walked amongst
the angels.

i believe we all find what we
are looking for underneath the
falling stars.
their dust is within us and we
have to trust our instincts
to not allow the temptations
of life
to overtake our soul, body
and minds.

after it is all said
and done. when the moon
has hung itself because
the sun never came back
up;
that is when i will stop
loving you. but not until
then.

the sun will always rise,
when i look into your eyes.

it was our scars that brought
you and i together.
they needed us to love each
other for them to finally
heal.

never again shall we be afraid
of what others may say or think
about our lives.
our story does not involve them,
nor will it ever make sense to
those who fail to understand
that scars will always be life
written on flesh.

they are simply words not
everyone can read.

she said, "all i want is to feel loved and
for the pain to go away. life has brought me
nothing but heartache and agony for the last
five years. hell, even my heart cries as the
nights pass without any sleep to speak of.
my father just passed away last week and my
mother recently disowned me. now i am going
to live with my aunt in new york city.
at least there i can see peace from my
window. they live on the 22nd floor and
lady liberty is within eye reach. i want
to be like her and stand tall against

and enemy. this world has beaten me
senseless and i cannot make any more
sense of this. will you please come
visit me?"

my tears were soaking into the carpet, before
my mouth even open. i told her. "i will.
i promise. i will see you in august and we can
visit the statue together." for the first time
in a long time a smile appeared on her face.
one that was part love and part relief. in the
end, we always needed each other, just as the
city needed lady liberty.

in the stillness of the night
is when i search to find the light;
illuminating from your eyes.

attracting my soul to venture
off into the dark; vetting for
love. i shall find them and when
i do, i will tell them hello
and how much i have missed seeing you.
-when the lights go out-

even if i had given her my
whole heart, i knew that
my soul would never
be enough.

a deafening silence filled
my lungs, as she left
with my last breath
of love.

in the end, all she wanted were
diamonds, but all i could
afford were the stars.
looking up at them now,
i still admire their beauty
and how priceless they
really are.

in a matter of what seemed like
seconds, she told me, "i will
wait for you."
with me choking back my tears,
i told her, "i will wait with you."
we both knew that this would be
tough, but in the end, what the
hell isn't tough about life?
we all make do with what we have,
yet somehow i knew i needed her to
survive. it's something about hearing
her voice in the night that stirs
my body with a concoction of elements
that even my soul cannot register.
my mind tells me, "before you close
your eyes, make sure you kiss her
goodnight." though she is not here
in person, i kiss the phone as we
hang up, just to let her know that

i will do whatever it takes for her
to realize, that through my eyes,
she epitomizes the life i need.

Underwater Mountains Publishing.
Elias Joseph Mennealy & Ryan Christopher Lutfalah.
A Private Company.

Made in the USA
San Bernardino, CA
07 May 2017